POETRY OF MY MIND

By Christopher J. Nesbitt

The poems I have wrote in this book are from my own experience in life as well as other people. I took my own perspective of situations as well as others and put it into different views. I hope you read and understand this book is not meant to harm anyone, but rather used as an outlet for me in my brightest and darkest times. If you need help, I hope you get whatever help you seek to find. I have gotten my own help, and it has inspired me to live a much greater life and accept things for what they are.

TABLE OF CONTENTS

Our Toxic Romance

Our love is fake,
Our love is real.
We touch to hurt,
We touch to heal.

We talk to fight
We talk to reflect.
We yell to scare
We yell to protect.

We run to get away,
We run into each other's arms.
We cry from the pain,
We cry from each other's charm.

We laugh at our emotions,
We laugh at our joys.
We hear the hate in our voices,
We hear our love through all the noise.

We see the disgust in our eyes,
We see the magic that we make.
Our love is real,
Our love is fake.

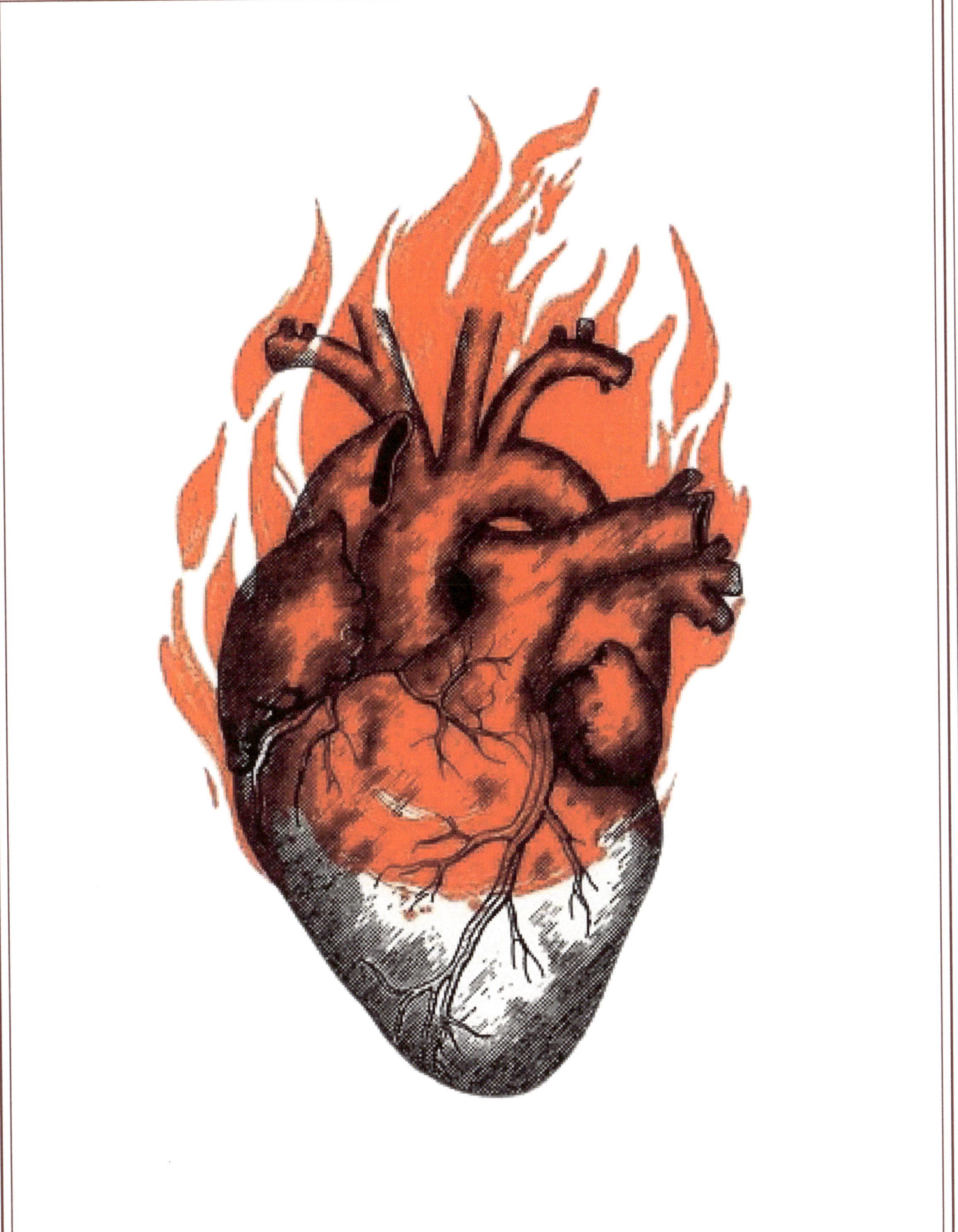

Before I

I lost my mind, but now it's found,
I learned to swim before I drowned.
I had to fall before I could fly,
I had to live before I could die.

I had to crawl before I could walk,
I had to listen before I could talk.
I had to learn before I could teach,
I had to understand the word before I could preach.

I had to love before I could hate,
I had to be on time before I was late.
I had to get hurt before I built a wall,
I had to lose you to know I had it all.

I love you

You're undoubtedly the love of my life,
I can't wait for you to be my wife.

I love you so much, like there's no tomorrow,
If it wasn't for you, I'd be in a world of sorrow.

My heart urns for you day in and day out,
You truly showed me what love is all about.

The man you deserve, I'm going to be for you,
To keep you by my side, I'll do whatever I have to do.

I love the softness of your skin and the gentleness of your touch,
You're the most beautiful woman I've ever seen; I love you so much.

Without you

I'm a ship lost at sea,
I'm a flower without a bee.

I'm a car with no fuel,
I'm a farmer with no mule.

I'm a lion without a roar,
I'm a bird who can't soar.

I'm a dolphin without a pod,
I'm a lawn without sod.

I'm an athlete without a sport,
I'm a charger without a port.

I'm a flag with no pole,
I'm a Deamon without a soul.

I'm nothing without you,
I need you, tell me what to do.

Dear Grandpa

Dear Grandpa, I know it's been a while,
I'm sure you're looking down, keeping me on file.
I look up to you and everything you did,
I wish I knew you as a man and not just as a kid.

I have a son, I named him after you,
I had to talk; I'm feeling kind of blue.
I know you'll listen; you were always good at that,
My boy is getting big; you should see him swing that bat.

Oh, by the way, Momma and Grandma say, "Hey,"
They say they love you and miss you every day.
Anyway, I just wanted to stop by,

I'll be looking for you in the sky.
I'm going to continue being the best man I can be,
Until we meet again, talk to God for me.

Grandpa Joe

You always kept spare change in your shoes,
Always had a pack on gum on you.
You tried to teach me tough love,
Now you're watching me from the stars above.

I hope heaven is great,
I want to tell you I love you, but I feel it's too late.
You were a warrior and had a tough fight,
All the advice you gave me, you were right.

Time heals wounds, but this never will;
When I think of you, I still get a cold chill.
It's been several years, and you're still on my mind,
You were always there; you were always kind.

*I miss you and never wanted you to go,
I ... I love you Grandpa Joe.*

Dear me

Dear me, how are you doing today?
How are you feeling? Are you okay?

Dear me, I know that life ain't always fun,
And it's okay to feel accomplished with everything you do.

Dear me, you've got to take things a day at a time,
Understand it's okay to tell someone you're in decline.

Dear me, it's okay to open up your heart,
And it's okay to let people go that don't play their part.

Dear me, I hope you know I'm proud,
And that it's okay to cry you're allowed.

Dear me, don't be afraid to let your voice be heard,
And that thinking you're alone is observed.

Dear me, don't fold your hand too soon,
And walk to the beat of your own tune.

Dear me, I hope you find the help you need,
And the voices in your head concede.

Have you

Have you buried someone you love?
Have you seen a missile fall from above?
Have you stared down the barrel of someone else's gun?
Have you been shot at trying to run?

Have you seen a bomb blow up your brothers?
Have you seen things you couldn't tell others?
Have you had a last breath left in your arms?
Have you responded to man-down alarms?

Have you seen a friend take their own life?
Have you given a flag to someone else's wife?
Have you seen blood hit the wall?
Have you heard a scream that made your skin crawl?

I've seen and done things I wish I never had to,
But have you?

I Never, I Will

I'll never be the guy in her love story,
I will be the man striving for glory.
I'll never be anyone's best man,
I will always stay true to who I am.

I'll never be the life of the party,
I will always do things right, never to harm me.
I'll never be the best looking in the room,
I will always find the truth, never assume.

I'll never be the person who lives without worry,
I will take my time with things and never hurry.
I'll never be the husband wives are jealous of,
I will always be victorious when push comes to shove.

I'll never love you like you love me,
I will always love you more than you'll ever see.

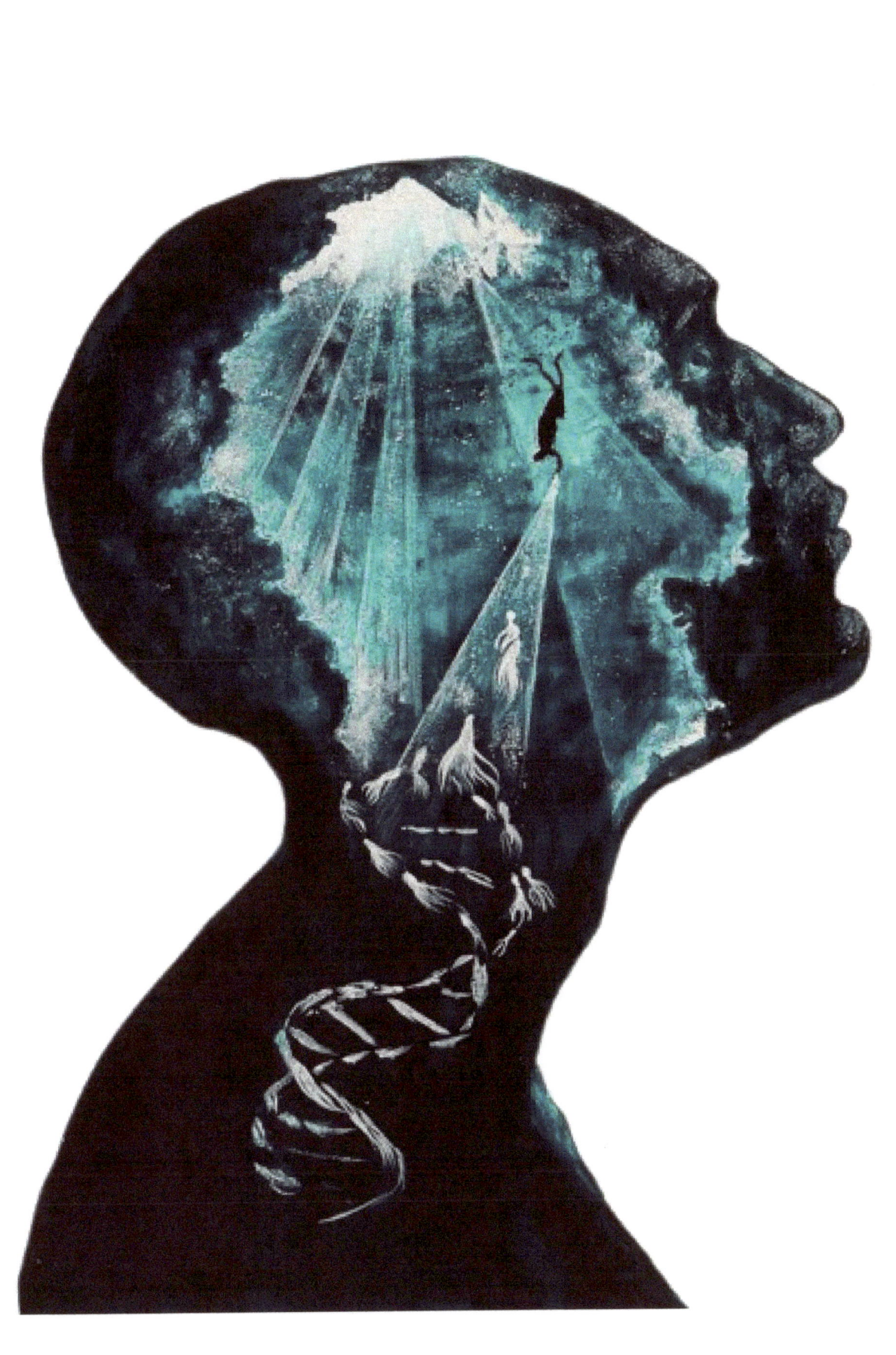

Me V.S. Myself

His reflection shows nothing but pain in his eyes,
You can see it all in every tear he cries.
He holds a past that he shields from the world,
If he told the ones he loved his life would be unfurled.

His heart is in shambles and he lives with a mask,
He struggles everyday focusing on a task.
The voices screaming in his head only he can hear,
Them escaping is his biggest fear.

His blood is always burning from anger kept inside,
He's felt all he can feel, there is no tear left to be cried.
How can he find peace?
He's confused on what to do...

The mirror is looking at him,
And I can see him too.

My Own Worst Enemy

I know I'm overthinking and for me that's easy to do,
But when I say "I love you" I don't hear "I love you too".
You're quick to get off the phone and end our conversation,
You say I'm in my own head but I have a funny sensation.

That you're done with us for good,
There are things I can live without, but you? I don't think I could
My heart aches at the thought of us apart,
I've always loved you, even from the start.

The thoughts of us ending and you finding someone new,
Makes me hate myself for what I never do.
I'm sorry for the way I am, I wish I could change,
My mind is battling itself with thoughts I exchange.

I'm sorry and I hope that I'm wrong,
I love you and without you I couldn't live long.

My Light

There's a light at the end of the tunnel
It's dim but bright enough to see,
The first step is the hardest one
I'm reaching out as darkness engulfs me.

As I move slow the path is harder to follow
The light grows big and then it gets smaller,
But the Lord is guiding me I must keep going
He's telling me to chase life, not the dollar.

I no longer need a path, just to listen to his voice
His word is good so I'm taking it to heart,
I'm not there yet
But me and the light are only an inch apart.

Let me

I love you baby
Let me kiss your lips,
Let me rest my hands
Directly on your hips.

Let me hold you
And make you feel safe,
Let me comfort you
Let me give you faith.

Let me whisper
Sweet things in your ear,
Let me make you secure
And eliminate your fear.

Let me show you
That our love is real,
Let me show you
Exactly how I feel.

Let me drop down
To a single knee,
Let me give you this ring
So forever we may be.

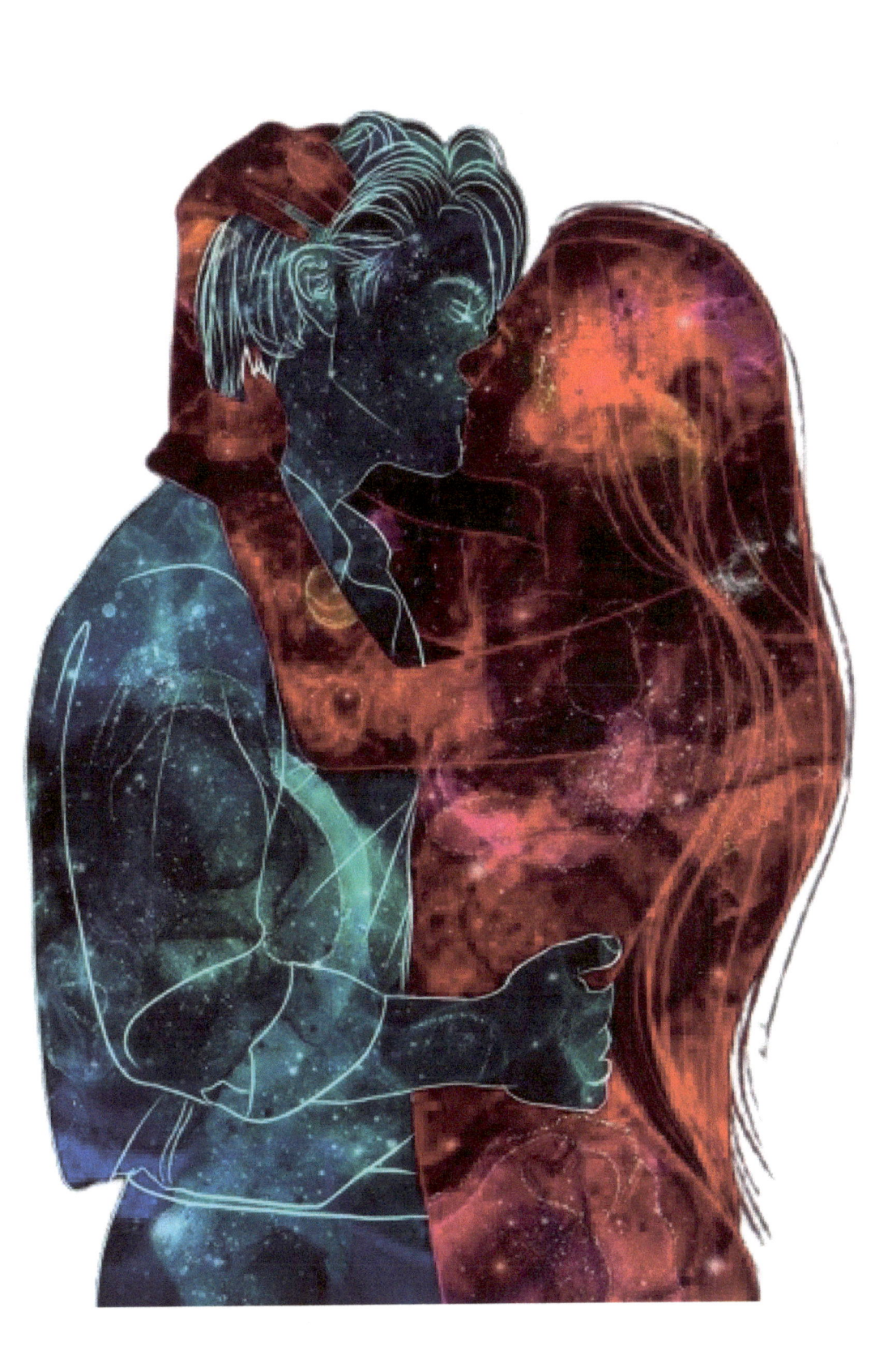

I do

Baby here's my last name
Let it be yours,
Having you as mine
Makes my heart soar.

Baby I know
You're the only one for me,
I'm going to treat you right
Baby you will see.

I want you to know
That I need your love,
To me you're and angel
Sent from above.

There's not a day
That I don't want you,
Baby here's my last name
I Do...

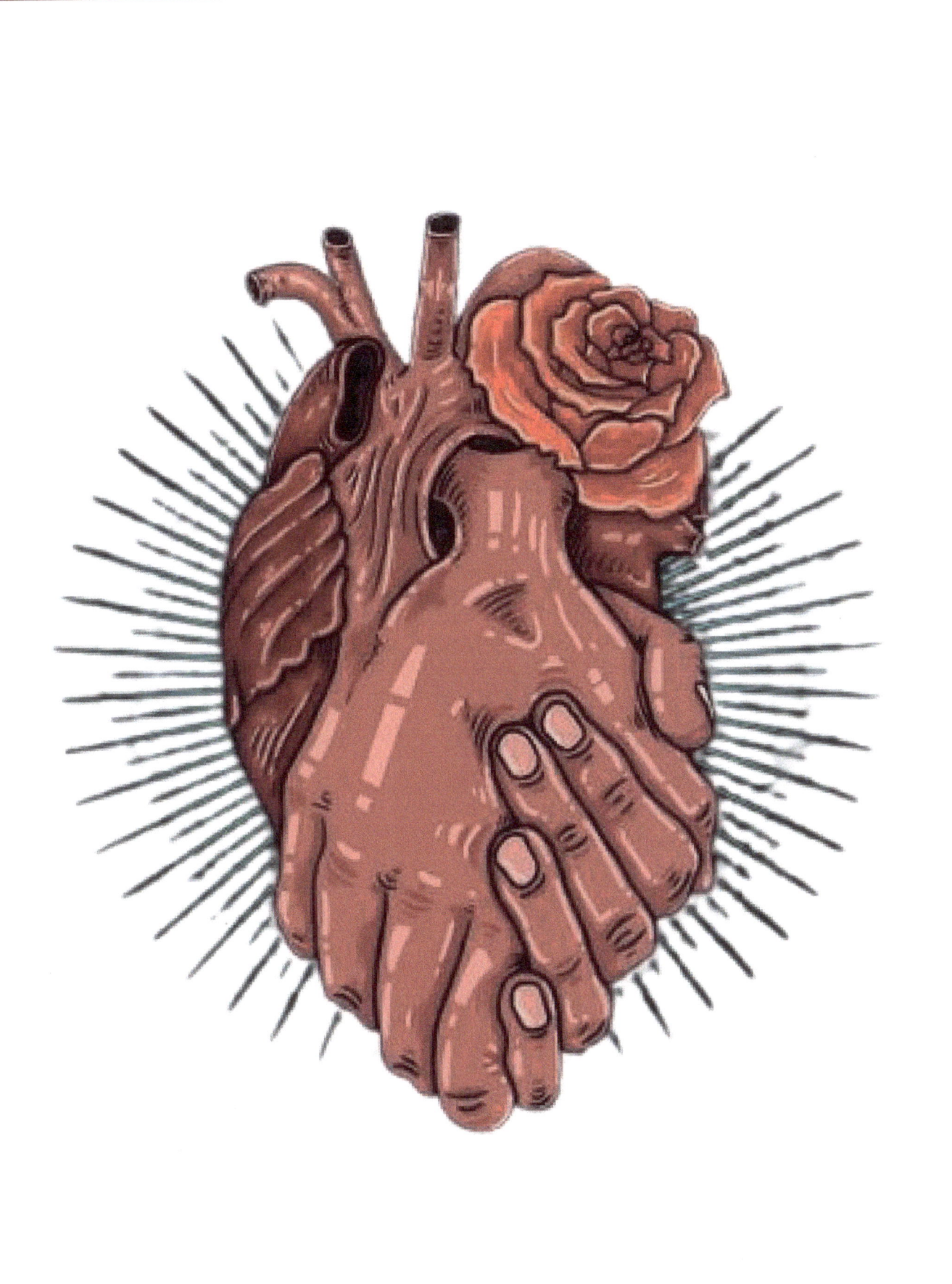

Set free

I've been saved
I've been set free,
From all the voices
That live inside me.

They've given up
They've finally conceded,
The Lord beat them down
And left them defeated.

He has blessed me
Gave me another chance,
In my mind
Only good thoughts dance.

He is my hero
I hope that he knows,
This chapter in my life
Is something I can close.

Tears For Her

With sadness in his eyes,
He looks at a picture of her and cries.
What happened to make her go away?
All he ever wanted was for her to stay.

Something about her changed,
Without her his life was rearranged.
Some wounds never heal,
He closes his eyes hoping this isn't real.

His whole body feels the pain,
His life is dark and full of rain.
The way he feels nobody will ever know,
Because on the outside his feelings don't show.

Only one knows this man and what he can see,
I know this man... It's me.

One Last Chance

I'm asking for one last chance
To prove I'm the man for you,
I know I messed up
And I haven't been true.

I don't know why I did it
I just want to take it back,
But I can't and I hurt you
That's just the fact.

I'm correcting my wrongs
Becoming a better man,
I'm doing it for us
I really am

I'm better for me
And that's important to you,
I know you don't trust it
But I'll work back to.

Just one last chance
That's all I ask,
I'm begging and pleading
Let's work past.

You...

Your color is beautiful
So wonderful and brown,
So full of love
All the way deep down.

Your hair is beautiful
In every style you choose,
When I kiss your lips
My love ensues.
Your eyes are so gorgeous
And full of life,
There's only one woman
I want as my wife.
Your hands are so soft
With every touch I feel,
You're so perfect
It feels surreal.
Your personality is priceless
So vibrant and joyful,
You are so true
Honest and Loyal.
There's so much love
That words can't describe,
You're my medication
No doctor could prescribe.

Am I?

Am I the kind that can't get right?
Am I the kind that wants to fight?
Am I the toxic one?
Am I the least favorite son?

Am I just a liar?
Am I happy living in the fire?
Am I hopeless or can I get help?
Am I denying how I felt?

Am I just garbage that needs to go to the dump?
Am I going to live or should I just jump?
Am I done living in hell?
Am I going to be, okay? Can you tell?

I want a way out I hope it comes soon,
Putting myself down is going to end in doom.

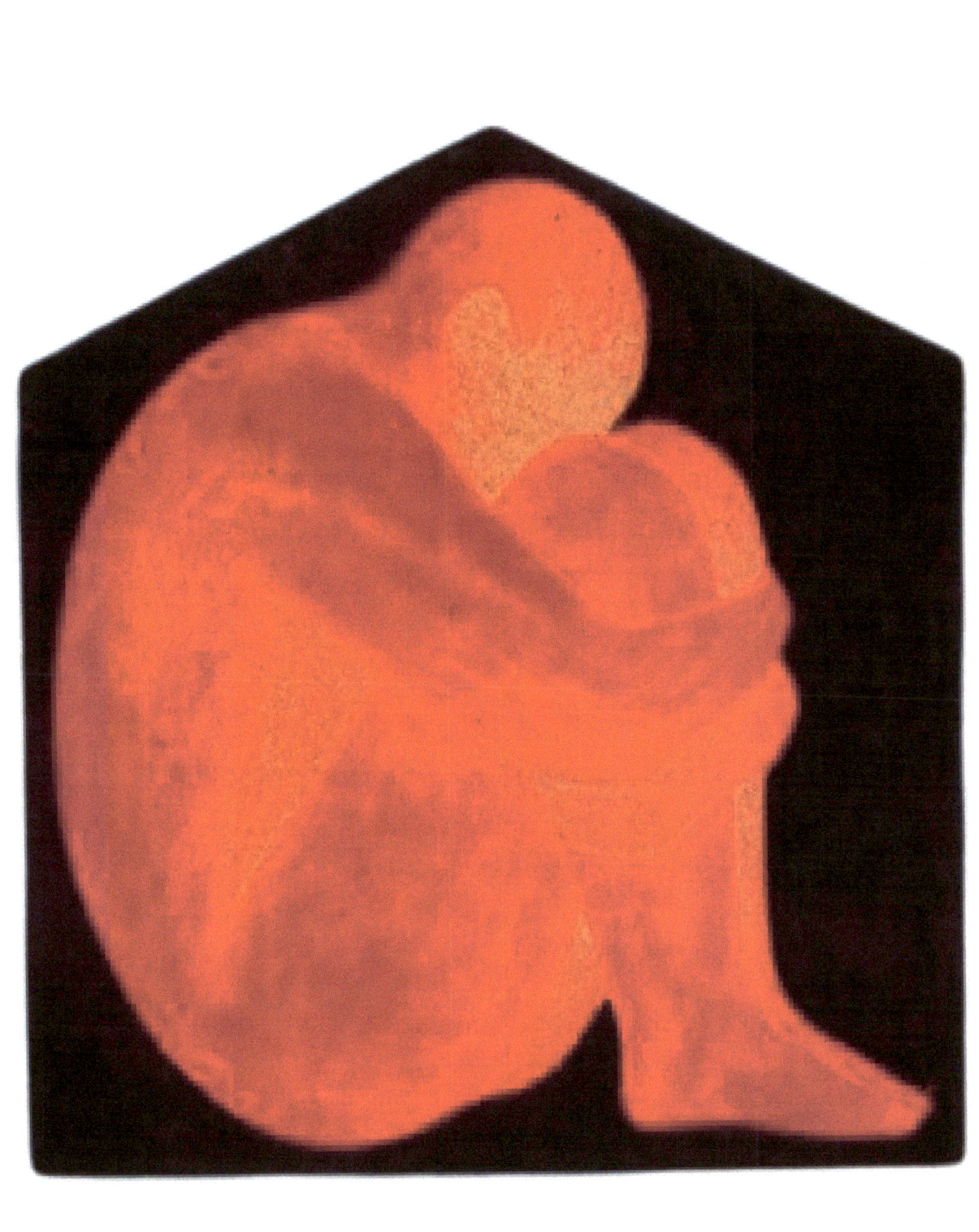

Voices

I'm sad and feel dead inside,
I want to feel better but I've tried and tried.
I just want to drink to heal my pain,
I've tried the sober life and there's nothing to gain.

I've called out to God but haven't heard back,
I just need a sign, I'm about to crack.
I miss the old me the one that wanted life,
No woman makes me feel like they can be a wife.

I hate each day that I get to breath,
I don't want to be here I just want to leave.
Please God just give me a sign,
To let me know its okay and everything is fine.

I can't take this much longer,
In my head these thoughts sit and ponder.
I wish they'd go away, why do they want me?
They won't listen, they won't leave me be.

I guess there's nothing else for me to do,
Time to listen to them and do what they want me to do.

You Make

You make my heart flutter like a butterfly,
You make me feel like a cloud in the sky.
You make my knees weak from your touch,
You make me feel a feeling I haven't felt much.

You make me want to give you the universe,
You make every bad thought disburse.
You make me happy like no one before,
You make me love you to my core.

You make me miss you when you're away,
You make me smile each and every day.
You make me tear up with joy in this life,
You make me delighted at the thought of you as my wife.

You make a difference just so you know,
You make my personality glow.
You make me know you're the one for me,
You complete me, I hope you see.

Me Without You

The earth without a sun,
A bullet without a gun.
A beach without sand,
A singer without a fan.

A baby without a mom,
A storm without the calm.
Liquor without the burn,
Ashes without an urn.

A traveler without somewhere to run from,
A church without a Nun.
A hoop without a ball,
My phone without your call.

My heart without someone to give it to,
Me Without You.

My Love

My pain is your gain,
My heart hurts while yours is aflame.
The anger set us apart,
We were doomed from the start.

Your love faded gray,
As I loved you more each day.
You held my heart and tore it to a shred,
I tried to sow it with a thread.

It was never good enough for you,
I loved you so much and you knew.
That was your weapon of destruction,
Loving you was the only way I could function.

The tears are gone, I know what to do,
Time to move on, I'm glad we're through.

Sleep Talking

Sleep talking, but it's the voices in my head,
They come awake when I'm asleep in bed.
Discussing everything they want to do,
People say I'm dreaming but they don't have a clue.

They show me things of evil every night,
To me its normal but to others they would fright.
No medication makes them go away,
They make it clear they are here to stay.

I tried to end myself but they won't let me do it,
They laugh at me and only speak elicit.
I hope to figure out exactly what they need,
So that these voices may finally concede.

Better Man

I don't know much but I know I love you,
To regain your trust, I know what I have to do.
I'll do whatever it takes to get back into your heart,
I can't stand the thought of being apart.

There will be setbacks like every change has,
But I will continue to do right, I know you're keeping tabs.
My change comes from within,
All I want is for us to win.

Whatever you need I'll give you my all,
I'm a better man and this time I'll answer the call.
You're perfect to me, I need you in my life,
So, take my hand, through struggle and strife.

You're the only one for me,
I hate we had to go through this for me to see.
But now my mind is clear,
Better days are near.

Inked Words

My pen touches paper
It's where my thoughts leak,
Writing down things
I wish I could speak.

My feelings come together
In ways that make rhymes,
Letting it out
Has saved me at times.

As words hit the paper
The ink sinks in,
Healing my pain
That I've built within.

Words of love
Words of hate,
Words of evil
Words that are great.

This is the way
I deal with my mind,
Battling my daemons
One pen stroke at a time.

War With Mind

Driving around town
I don't want to go home,
It's a full house
But I'm all alone.

No one understands
No one gets me,
I've been through a lot
Seen things I didn't want to see.

So, when I'm home
I have to act okay,
But deep down inside
I struggle getting through the day.

Maybe if you knew
Maybe you could help,
Maybe if you knew
You could understand what I felt.

What if I'm judged
What if family don't care,
What if you hate me for it all
This isn't fair.

I'm in a war with my mind
No piece in sight,
I've got to go away
I think I just might.

Am I Just a Number

Am I really just a number in your phone,
If so then who are really with when you say you're alone.
How much time do I have to waste for you to give me the truth?
I won't wait forever for you I'm still in my youth.

Yeah, I love you but I've said that before,
Just another heartbreak, I'm about to close the door.
Living this lie really hits me hard,
This shit you feed me is just the "I'm playing you card".

You got me good at first, I was convinced,
I'm sure your heart is fine but mine is minced.
All the "feelings" you have damn sure don't show,
But I'm slowly not giving a shit just so you know.

I wonder

Sometimes I wonder what goes on in your head,
Sometimes I wonder why you leave me on read.
If there's another guy give it to me straight,
If you don't love me, tell me don't make me wait.

If I whisper in your ear, does it make your heart rush?
When I say you're beautiful does it make you blush?
If I died tomorrow, what would you do,
Turn around and cry or think I was a fool.

When you look into my eyes what do you really feel,
I'm dedicating my life to you just tell me if its real.
When I kiss your lips does it make your heart melt?
The first time I said "I love you" tell me how you felt.

I'm a guy, my feelings don't show the same,
Tell me this is real and not another game.

The Roast

It's four in the morning and I'm twisted,
Damn girl you called? I guess I just missed it.
You're an ex for a reason, you want to get back with me?
I'm denying all your calls, woman, can't you see?

I don't want to see your pictures I'm trying not to gag,
You don't need more make-up you need a bag.
Put your clothes back on I don't want to see that mess,
Trick I don't want you, is it that hard to guess?

You think you look good with your eyebrows on "fleek"
Change your name to clown, you look like a freak.
Is it a holiday? Because you're about to get this roast,
Everybody raise your glass even the ugly ones deserve a toast.

So, here's to you and all your thotty ways,
Between those legs ... the highway has had slower days.

Rebound

I'm drinking at the bar
Trying to get over you,
I found a girl
I'm going to take her home to.

You done me wrong
And I've got the proof,
Or at least 90 percent of it
We're about to blow this roof.

I'm rebounding tonight
I should be the MVP,
I don't want you back
Baby you'll see.

If I learned one thing in life
It's what goes around comes around,
Your turns coming up
I hope it gets you down.

I hope you're happy
Enjoying your new man,
Have the time of your life
Because without you I know I can.

Alone

I look left, I look right, but nobody's around,
I'm trying to scream but I'm not making a sound.
I want to be home but don't know where to go,
I'm lost in this world and submerged in everything I know.

I feel pain every day and it hurts to my core,
I want to feel love but I don't know how anymore.
Happiness is just a thought and not something I feel,
I wear some things on my sleeve but most I conceal.

I want to let someone in but fear they will leave,
All this weight makes it hard to breath.
I'm trying to hold on to the will to keep moving,
But every time I get up, I keep losing.

I'm trapped in my own head with these thoughts and nightmares,
I'm almost out of hope I've shot out my last flares.
My own darkness terrifies me like no tomorrow,
I need someone... please help carry my sorrow...

My Wrong

I know I did you wrong,
And I know I've done it for so long.
I know there's no excuse for my behavior,
But if I can, can I ask you for a favor?

Could you look deep down to forgive me?
Everything in the past can we leave it be?
I hope you can take my sorrow and understand it,
Not accept it, but think about it a little bit.

I know I'm the reason for all the pain,
It's me single handed, there's no one else to blame.
I know that if I can see the sun through the rain,
Then hopefully one day you could do the same.

I want you to know I never meant to make your heart hurt,
I betrayed you and took away your comfort.
I'm sorry all the way to my core,
I made you sad and hurt but won't anymore.

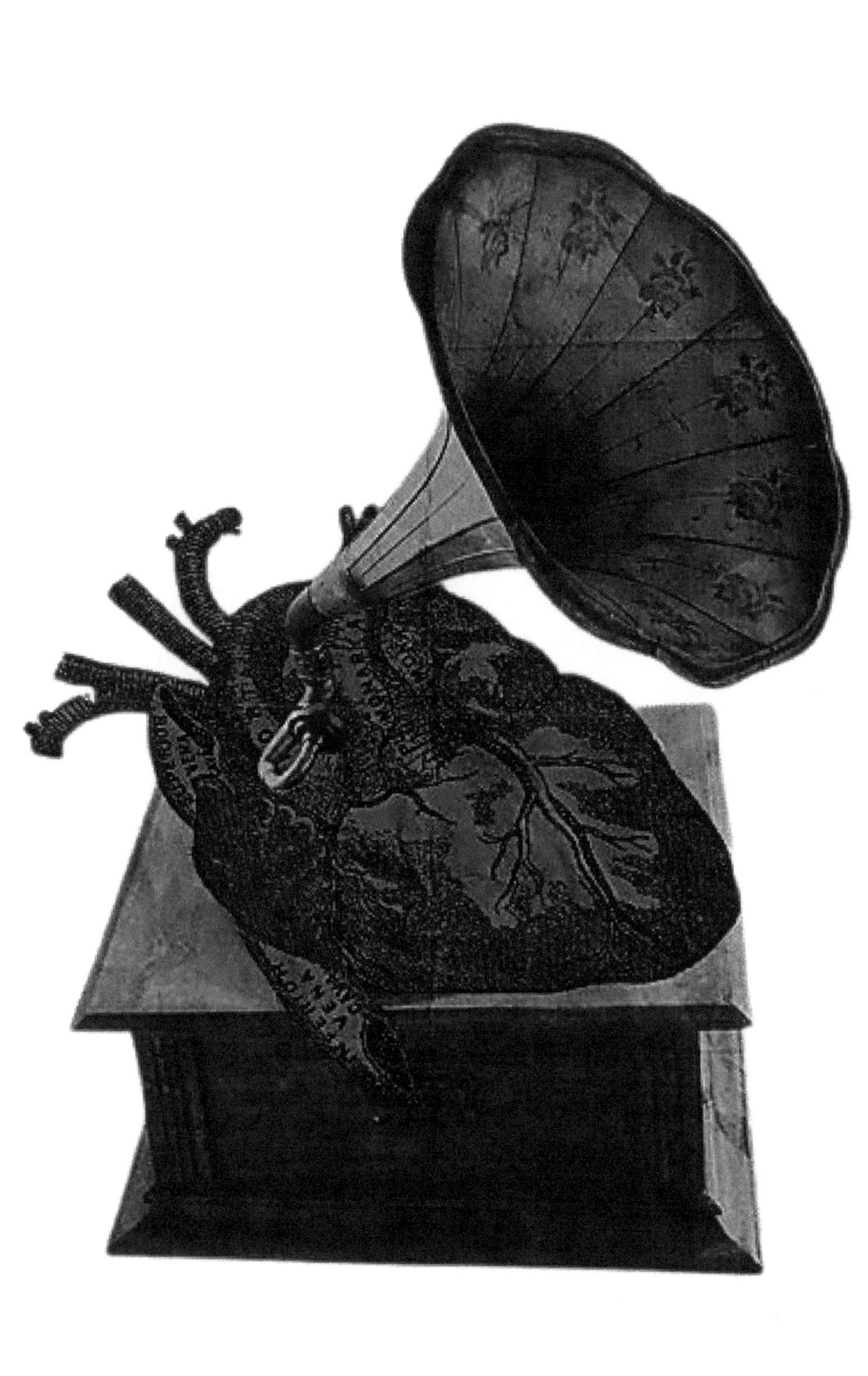

Never Out of Mind

Out of sight but never out of mind,
You're the person I'm trying to leave behind.
You make it hard to trust and hard to love,
Getting over you I need some help from above.

I keep asking myself why I wasn't enough,
The truth may hurt but I promise I'm tough.
My heart is broke and full of despair,
I guess I was wrong thinking we could fair.

I've only wanted you for the rest of my life,
We were supposed to be forever with you as my wife.
There's a constant ache knowing I'm not the man you desire,
It grows larger knowing you're the only woman I'll admire.

I wish you knew my pain but it's like you don't care,
I'd love you to walk in my shoes but I know you wouldn't dare.

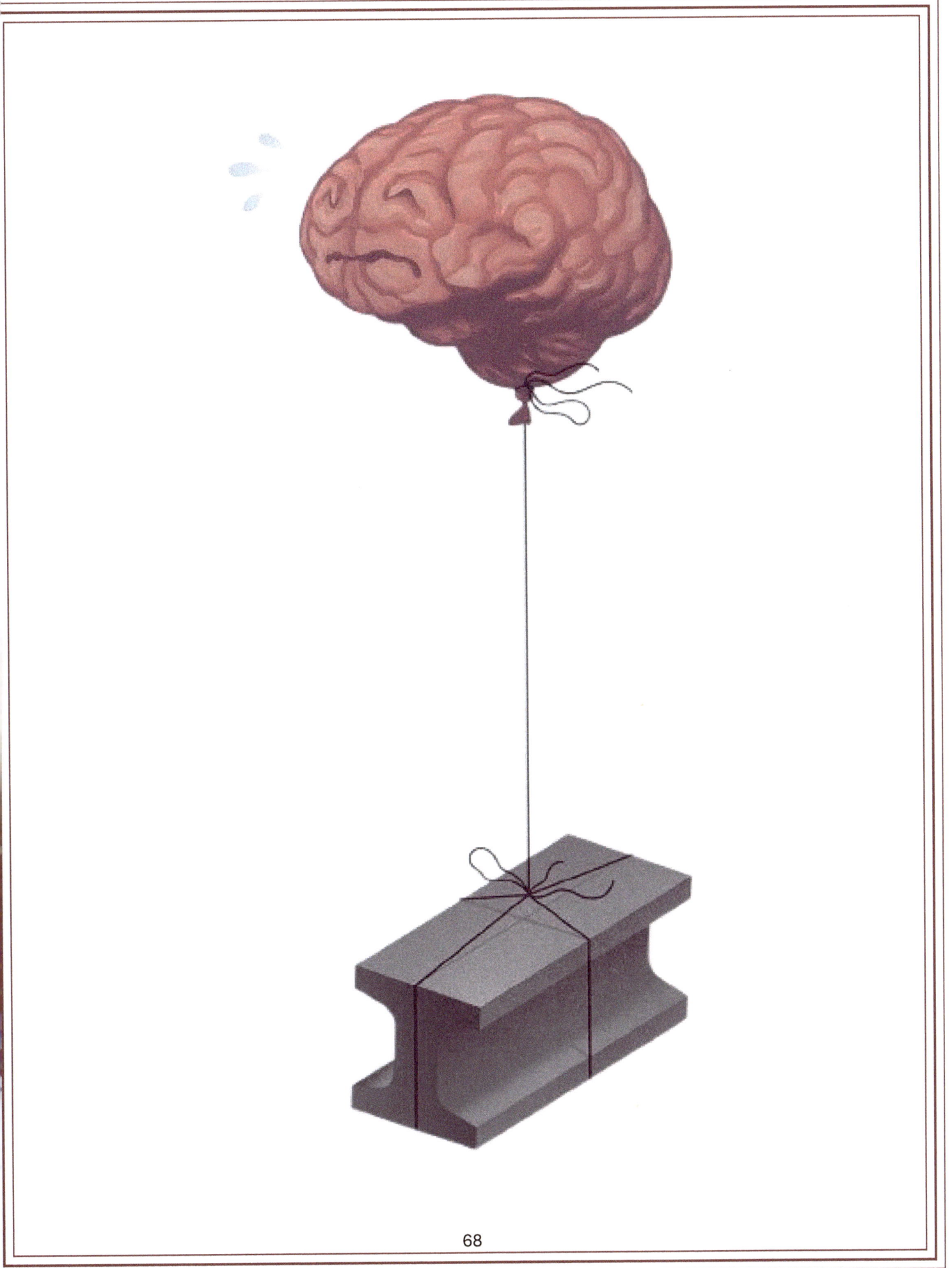

The Worst Trauma

I didn't know him well I seen him in passing,
He was usually hanging out talking and laughing.
The problem with the military is you've got to feel nothing,
But how do you hold it in without combusting.

After a while he wasn't acting the same,
I wish I knew what he had going on in his brain.
I remember walking by hearing him cry,
While screaming through his pillow "I wish I would die".

For a while I never understood taking your own life,
Kids with no father and a widowed wife.
That day on watch his weapon was an M-4,
He looked at me, flipped it around, and his life was no more.

The memory is burnt into my head,
I'm guilted every day I couldn't help him instead.
I'll never forget the sound and seeing his body hit the ground,
While a pool of blood circled around.

I'm sorry I couldn't help and I relive it every day,
Until I see you again, I'll continue to pray.

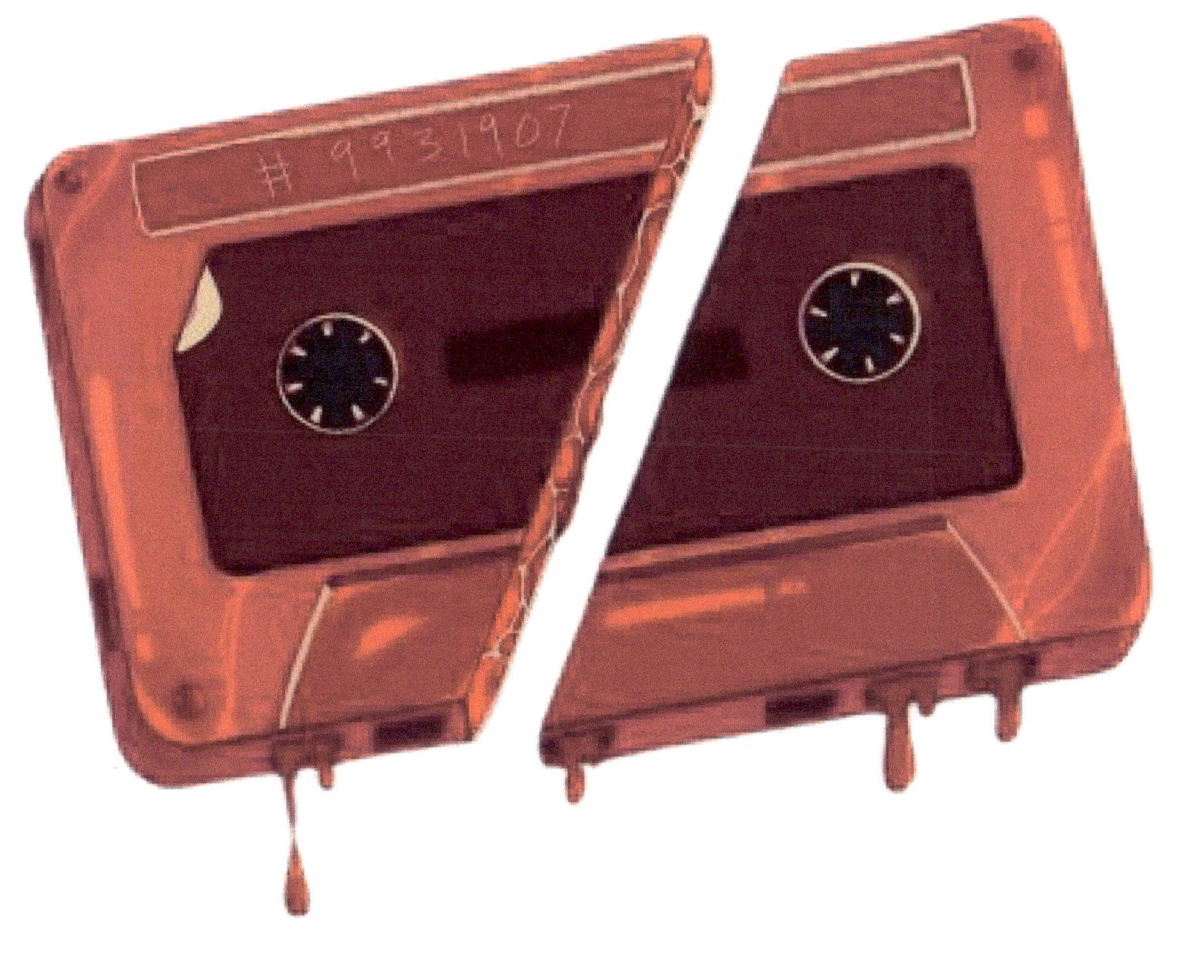

Another Nightmare

Another nightmare to relive the hurt,
Keeping me up all night on high alert.
The voices, the screaming ringing in my head,
I lay here awake wishing I was dead.

I think about you more than you could know,
But it's what I seen when you decided to go.
I weep for you till there is no tear left to fall,
You could have talked to me; I would've answered the call.

I ask myself if it's my fault I didn't reach out,
To this day I still don't know what it was all about.
I know I shouldn't but I take the blame,
There's been a few times I've attempted the same.

Maybe I can't because I'm too scared,
Or the regret knowing people cared.
I just want to say I miss you I wish I could've done more,
I hate myself for your loss down to my core.

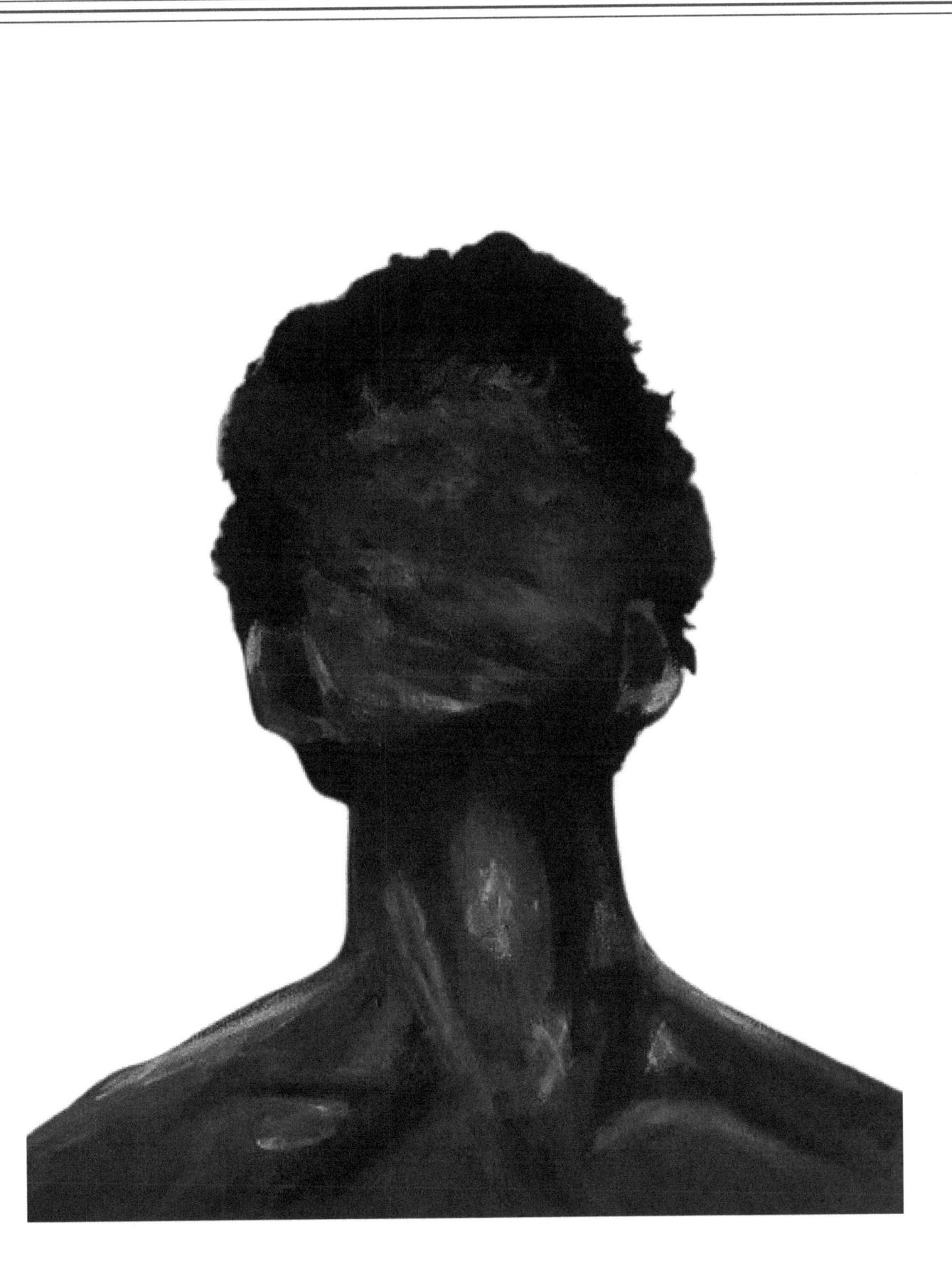

Life

Somedays I wish I was six feet in the dirt,
Because I don't want to deal with the pain and the hurt.

The trauma I remember since I was a baby,
And the trauma when I was overseas in the Navy.

The sexual abuse I had to withstand every day,
I didn't want to do it but I didn't know what to say.

To say the least my sister's dad was an evil man,
Hed rape me and even beat me with a pan.

I was overpowered to small to defend myself,
Hed tell me not to make a noise or else.

At the age of 13 I finally spoke up, I wasn't scared,
My mother came to my rescue because she's the only one who cared.

I decided to join the Navy after graduation,
I was sent to Sasebo Japan Naval Station.

Where I witnessed the death of a fellow service member,
He took his own life sometime before December.

I know the date but I hate to recall it,
It led me to alcohol I had to get.

The depression led to trying to take my own life.
I would've never had a son or a future wife.

But it led me to a place where I can find peace and joy,
Instead of ending my life and the hearts id destroy.

Intoxication

Crack a bottle light a smoke,
Turning in my coin because you took me as a joke.
Drowning in the bottle just like you want,
It's hard not to see all the dirty laundry you try not to flaunt.

All the lies you told to make me stay,
And all the toxicity I had to obey.
I just wish I knew I wasn't the only one,
You're the reason I'm holding this bottle and this gun.

I've never loved someone like I do you,
But you decided to do what you always do.
Act like you care but have someone on the side,
I'm a fool for thinking we were forever, like you were down to ride.

You brought the old me back I hope you're happy with your choices,
You made it too easy to welcome back the thoughts and the voices.
The bourbons got me blurry its 2 AM on the clock,
I'm starting to accept this taste I'm getting for my Glock.

With my finger on the trigger, I'm ready for my fate,
My tour of life ends on this date.

My Future

Her eyes are the perfect shade of brown,
She knows how to pick me up when I'm down.
Her skin is so beautiful and smooth,
Her voice is understanding as it soothes.

Her smile lights up the room,
When she says "I love you" it sends me to the moon.
She's got a body that drives me insane,
Her personality is sweeter than sugar cane.

Her lips are softer than cotton,
Everything she's done for me will never be forgotten.
She's gorgeous in every way,
I love her, I'm going to marry her someday.

Whiskey Downs

I'm six shots deep, I'm feeling good,
I know I shouldn't drink but I think I should.
The poison keeps me in a loop,
Spinning my vision like a Hoola-Hoop.

The pain goes away with every sip I take,
I love these feelings but they're all fake.
I promised myself I'd quit but I failed,
I'm off my tracks, I've been derailed.

Just one more shot I swear I'll quit this time,
My mood is going up it's starting to climb.
But what goes up must come down,
I know what happens when I drink brown.

I start to think of you and what I did,
I was reckless acting like a kid.
I punish myself everyday for the actions I took,
I was dishonest and disloyal and had you shook.

I love you, I'm sorry please don't go,
I need you in my life more than you could know...

My Savior

I talked to God today
He finally spoke to me,
He said "it'll all be okay,
Don't overthink let things be".

I prayed like I never have before
Giving him all my heart and burden,
Opened my Bible
Sat and watched the sermon.

Like it says in Isaiah 40:31
I have hoped in the lord and renewed my strengths,
I trust in him with every decision that I make
Being loyal to him I go to great lengths.

He helped me find love in myself,
Find love in others,
Love thy self and love thy neighbor
Treat people like sisters and brothers.

In you, Lord, I have taken refuge
Let me never be put to shame,
I've given in and have been saved
I Love him deeply; I know he feels the same.

I Know, But I Know

I know I love you but you're not good,
I cannot leave you, but I know I should.
I know our lives are complete with one another,
But the hurt is to great having each other.

I know everyone thinks we're meant to be together,
But I know we can't lie to ourselves forever.
I know the life we've built has been a blast,
I know our last fight won't be our last.

I know that we can live happily ever after,
But I know that our past has been a disaster.
I know that were good,
But I know that we're no good.

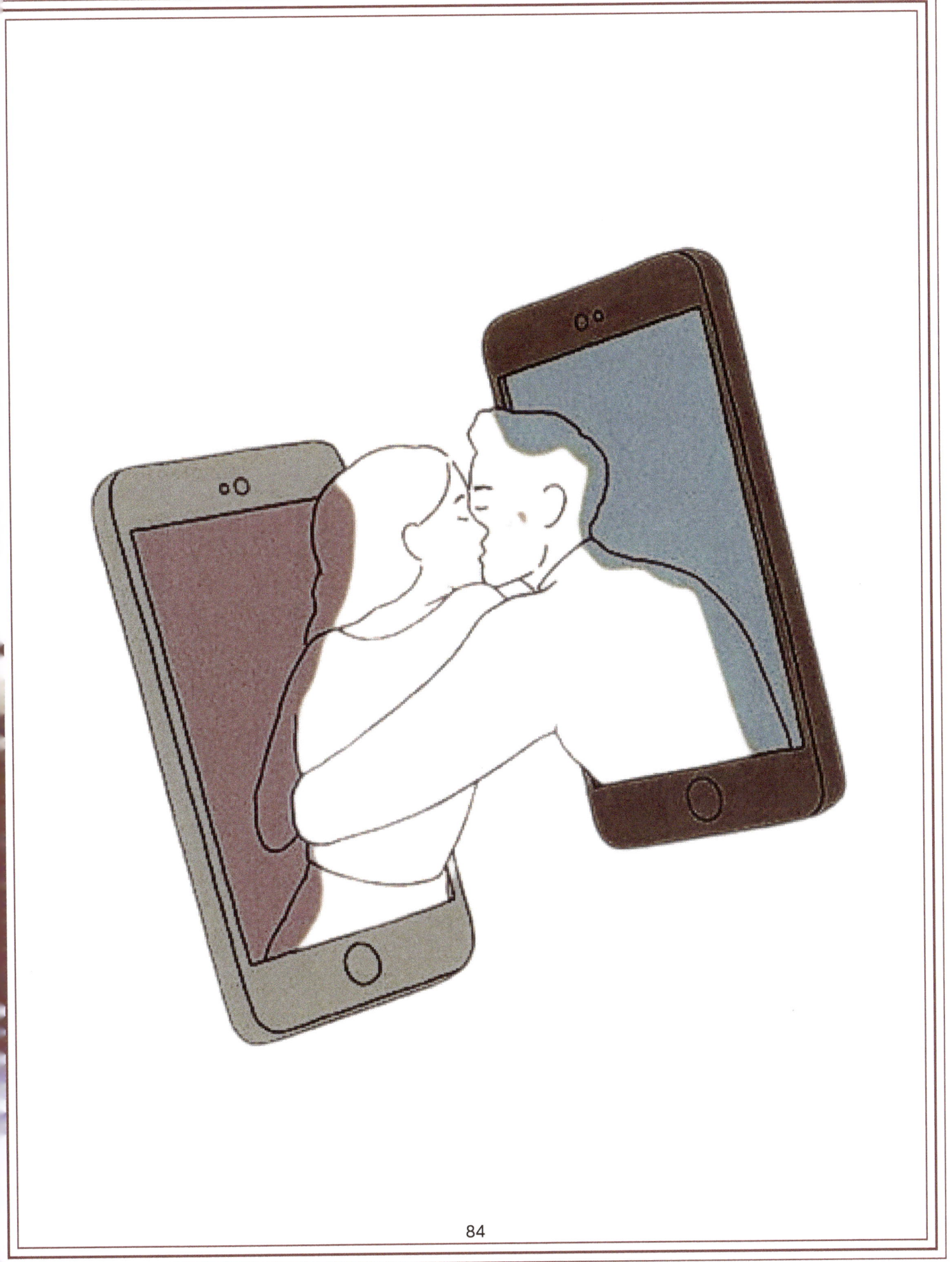

Saved

Had to hit rock bottom so I could start looking up,
Had to change the way I viewed my cup.
My glass is half full not empty,
Had to scare the daemons so they don't tempt me.

I'm on the path to salvation,
Lord lead me away from temptation.
If I can be saved then so can you,
Just trust in the Lord with everything you do.

The verses in the book help me see,
That each days a gift and he cares about me.
I chose to find God because my life needed change,
Things were going bad, and it was time to rearrange.

I had to get off the bottle and stay true to him,
I'd rather love him than live in sin.

The End

I don't want to be alive,
I can't handle the thoughts in my head that thrive.
I want someone to jump in and see what I see,
I want someone to see what it's like to be me.

When something is going well, I must ruin it,
My anger is like a flame that's always lit.
Just a little fuel to my fire and I'm another person,
I feel like my condition will only worsen.

I've come to accept with a clean and sober mind,
I want to die, hang in the woods where no one will find.
I hate myself and everything I do,
I want everyone to accept my wishes too.

I need a gun, some pills, or a rope,
I'd rather be dead than sit around and mope.
My Son will find a father much better than me,
I'm not a good man and that's what I want him to be.

Just like she says, "I'm a sad excuse for a man",
I agree... I must follow through with my plan.
Lord take my last breath and give it to someone in need,
I'm going soon whether it's you or me doing the deed.

Time For Change

His heart is cold yet full of regret,
The man in the mirror has not forgiven him yet.
All the wrongs he's trying to correct,
He's had nothing but time to reflect.

He hates himself and others feel the same,
He's done nothing but tarnish his own name.
He's set up his life to be alone,
All his mistakes he has to own.

Change starts with forgiving oneself,
Doing all the right things for your own health.
While he forgives himself for his past,
He hopes to take things slow and not fast.

The mirror creates a smile,
He's been working on himself for a while.
He no longer judges himself for what he's done,
Now he can start being better for his son.

He knows the man he wants to see,
He knows what to do and who to be.

My Rock

As you hold me in your arms
I can finally be weak,
I need you to be strong for me
Without you my life would be bleak.

I'm grateful I have you
For you to be my rock,
I hope you know I love you
You have my heart on lock.

You make my life
Full of pleasure,
What I feel for you
No one can measure.

You have a benevolent personality
You have a heart of gold,
You have breathtaking beauty
My love for you will never grow cold.

Dear God

Dear God
Am I living right?
Am I doing, okay?
Am I in your sight?

I ask questions
Because in not sure,
Even though I'm older
I still act immature

I look for your guidance
A lot more these days,
You impact my life
In the best of ways.

I know you're listening
It helps me get through,
The toughest of times
Having faith in you.

Having your love
Means the world to me,
I'm trying to do better
I know you can see.

Only If You're

I can only be a King
If you're my Queen,
I can only be an Actor
If you're my scene.

I can only be a husband
If you're my wife,
I can only be happy
If you're in my life

I can only be a dad
If you're the mom,
I can only be the Morning
If you're my Dawn.

I can only be Clyde
If you're my Bonnie,
You're my other half
You complete me.

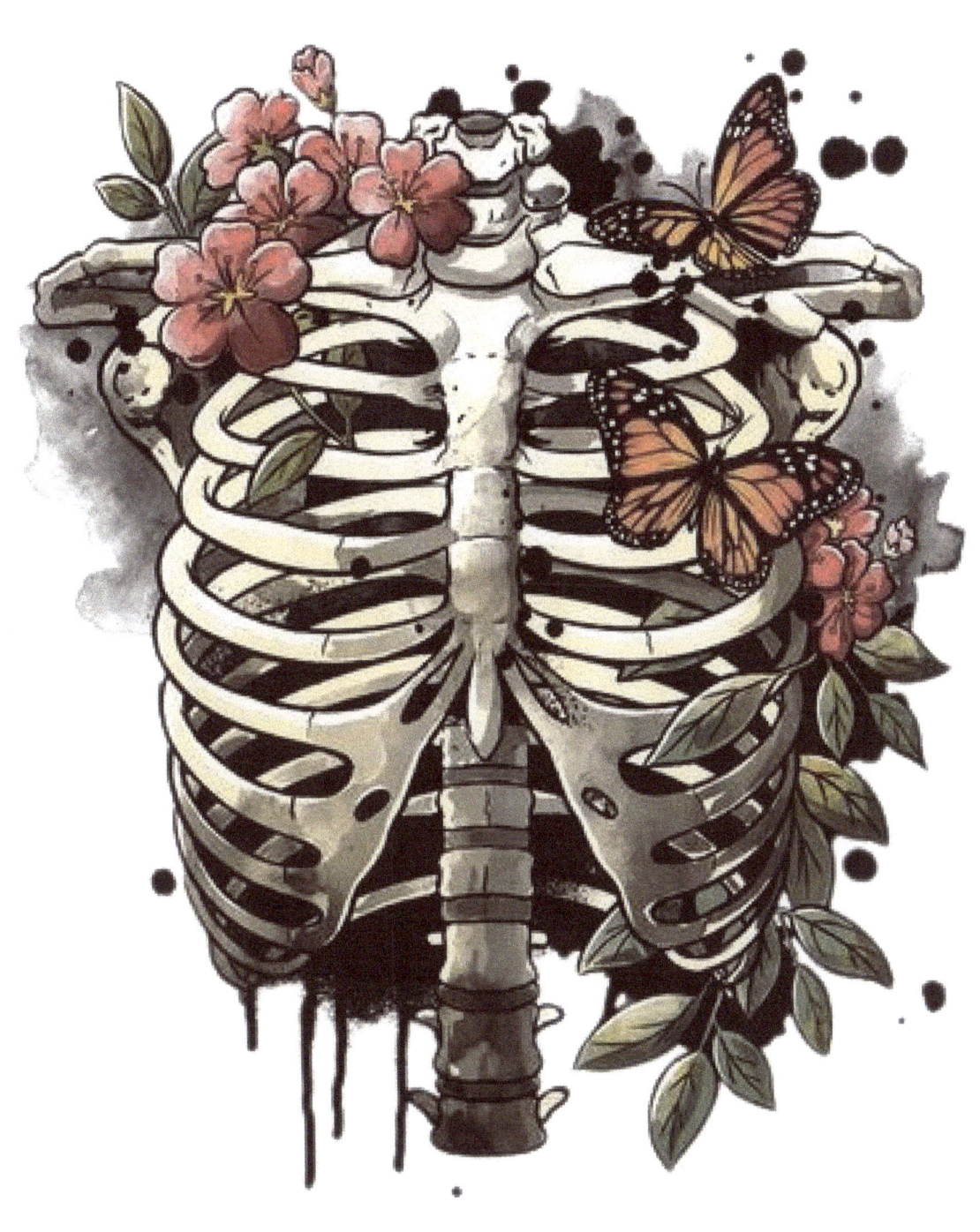

Pop That Seal

Burning feeling as it rolls through my body,
At this point drinking feels like a hobby.
I'm addicted to the feeling of feeling nothing at all,
I drink to drown my pain, and sleep where I fall.

From sunup to sundown I'm emptying the bottle,
Swerving these backroads, I'm nearing full throttle.
This jar of this lightning really hits the spot,
Slowly blurring out my past of things I haven't forgot.

Time goes by when you ain't having fun,
Holding this bottle might as well be my gun.
Tears on your picture and on your ring,
I haven't been the same since you threw that thing.

Lord, I know I ain't living right,
But I'm just trying to get through the night.
The morning son is too bright,
But I got my next bottle in sight.

Taking one more drink to heal,
Keep running out, so I keep popping that seal.

We Want

We want acres and acres of woods in sight,
We want love that lasts more than one night.
We want faith that never goes away,
We want people never to lead us astray.

We want a happy home,
We want to never be alone.
We want the ups and downs in life,
We want to keep going through the struggle and strife.

We want to never worry about money,
We want our days to be sunny.
We want to make it together,
We want each other forever.

Bigger Man

Wasting time with the blue mountains
Another heartbreak dragging on,
One more silver bullet
Another girl done me wrong.

I don't want to feel
I want to be numb,
Beer after beer
Another shotgun.

She left me
High and dry,
So, I keep drinking
Just trying to get by.

I thought it was love
But I guess it was a sham,
So, goodbye to you
I'll be the bigger man.

I Stopped, I Started

I stopped drinking
I stopped lying.
Started thinking
And started trying.

I stopped being angry at the world
I stopped being sad,
I started listening
And I started being a better dad.

I stopped cheating
I stopped mistreating you,
I started being honest
And started being true.

I stopped hating life
I stopped being what others wanted me to be,
I started understanding
And I started loving me.

Never Walk Away, Please Stay

You took my love as a joke,
Took my heart and beat it till it broke.
You chewed me up and spit me out,
I'm glad I know what you're all about.

You were my love till money walked by,
I wasn't your forever; I was just another guy.
I hate you; I love you; why am I still here?
My blurry eyes make it hard to see clear.

I hope he was worth it, the man of your dreams,
When you tell him how you feel I hope he knows what it means.
You're evil, you make the devil look good,
Hell is waiting on your arrival just like it should.

But yet I want you, I need you, please don't go away,
I hope you know every day,
I kneel by my bed and pray,
That just maybe you'll stay,
And never walk away.

Ultimate Sin

On that night the trees
We're whistling in the wind,
That's where I seen
The worst sin ever sinned.

The sky was gray
And full of depression
That is where I learned
My greatest lesson.

Life is precious
don't take things for granted,
and don't harm yourself
like God commanded.

There's never a struggle
You must battle alone,
If you allow God
In your heart and in your home.

My Son

I want you to know,
Daddy is doing his best,
I need you to be better than me
That is my only request.

Seeing you smile
Changes my whole mood.
I love everything about you
Even your little attitude.

Seeing you grow
Is the best gift I could ask for,
I know you'll do great things
I believe you can soar.

I love you
But words can't describe,
How I really feel
All the way inside.

Momma

I'm beaming that
I can call you mom,
When I'm upset
You know how to calm.

There's nothing I could do
To payback everything you've done,
All I can do
Is try to be the best son.

It took a while
But now I understand,
Your strength as a mother
And your ability to withstand.

I love you,
You're the best mom ever,
I will cherish our time
Because we don't have forever.

Let Her Go

With a tear in his eye,
He looks at her and says goodbye.
Not till later, but for good,
He wants to chase after her but don't know if he should.

All the misery they've caused each other,
All the fights one after another.
The screaming and yelling are no good for them,
All the hate when they condemn.

He tries to deny the fact he still loves her,
He's trying to forget about everything they were.
He wishes things would change,
But all their anger they exchange.

He knows he needs her, but he must let go,
As she turns away his emotions start to show.
He chases after her car, but it's too late,
Being apart is now their fate.

Do You

Do you ever wish you were truly happy?
Do you live for catastrophe?
Do you want peace?
Do you have a way to release?

Do you want war?
Do you know what you'd die for?
Do you have love?
Do you have someone watching from above?

Do You have lust?
Do you have someone you can trust?
Do you dwell on things you can't change?
Do you talk to someone when you feel estrange?

Do you live a life with sobriety?
Do you struggle with anxiety?
Do you live free?
Or are you stuck in your own mind like me...?

Heartbroken

I failed in life
I failed with us,
I love you
But, there's nothing left to discuss.

I'm heartbroken
That you don't want this anymore,
I guess I didn't try hard enough
All the signs I tried to ignore.

It's me
I'm the problem,
I'm fixing my issues
I can solve them.

You're my heart
It destroys me your leaving,
Doing life without you
Makes me want to stop breathing.

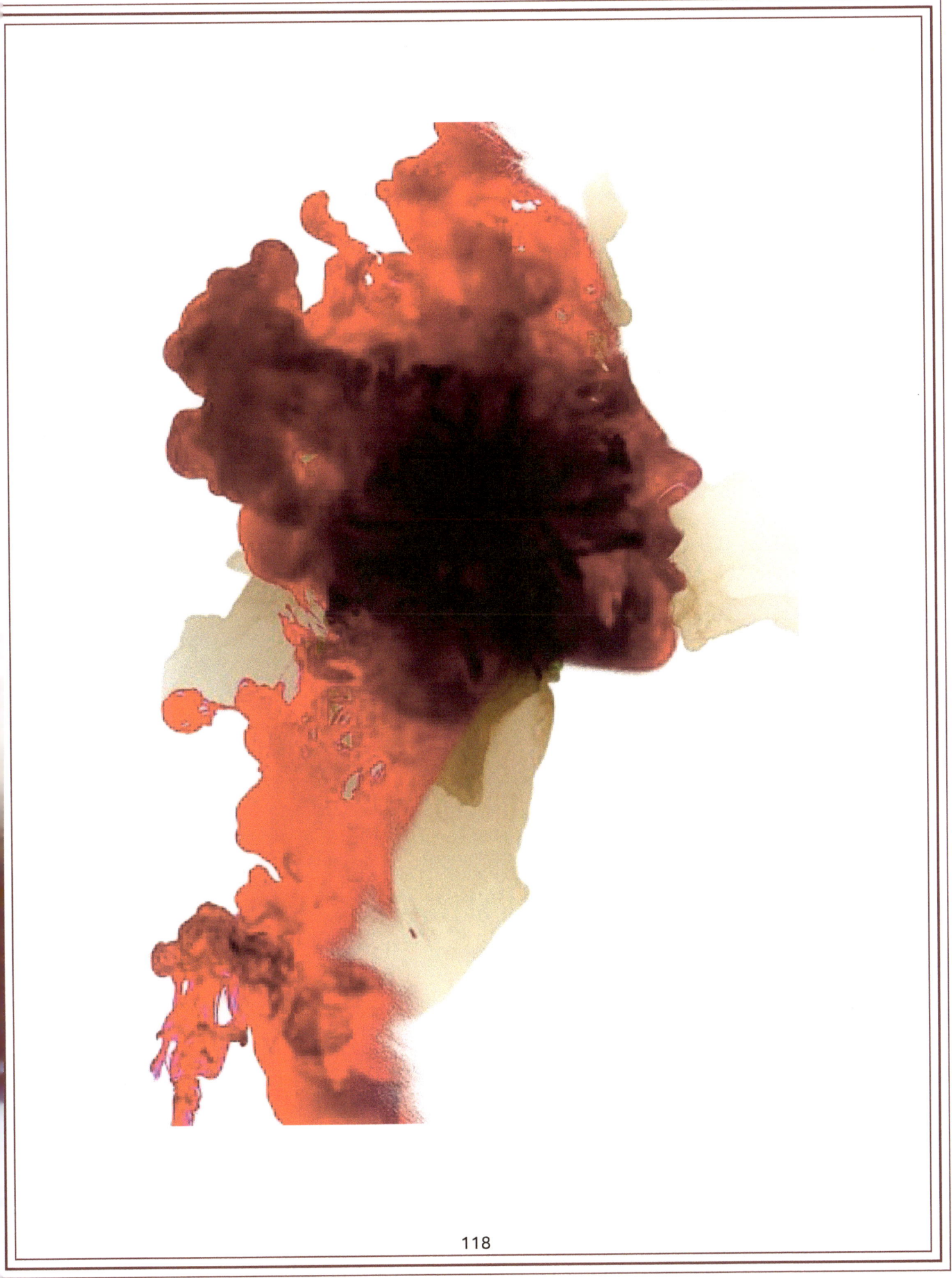

You Have, You Are

You have my heart
You have my soul,
With you
My life is whole.

You have my truth
You have my all,
Whenever you need me
I'll answer the call.

You are my other half
You are my queen,
You are the most beautiful woman
I've ever seen.

You are my everything
You are the love of my life,
I'll love you forever
Will you be my wife?

She Loves Me, She Loves Me Not

She loves me
She loves me not,
I always wonder
I always have this thought.

Picking pedals
Off of roses,
Thinking how her heart
Opens then closes.

Red pedals
Hit the ground,
So quiet
They don't make a sound.

The truth in your feelings
Is what I sought,
She loves me
She loves me not.

My Anger

When I let my anger show,
It makes my trouble grow.
If I could just think,
I wouldn't let myself sink.

If only I knew,
Exactly what to do.
I want to explode,
My glass is overflowed.

I just want to yell and scream,
I wish this was just a dream.
I'm on the brink of losing my mind,
I keep searching for help, I can't seem to find.

Am I going insane?
I can't deal with all this pain.
I feel like I'll be in danger,
If I can't defuse my anger.

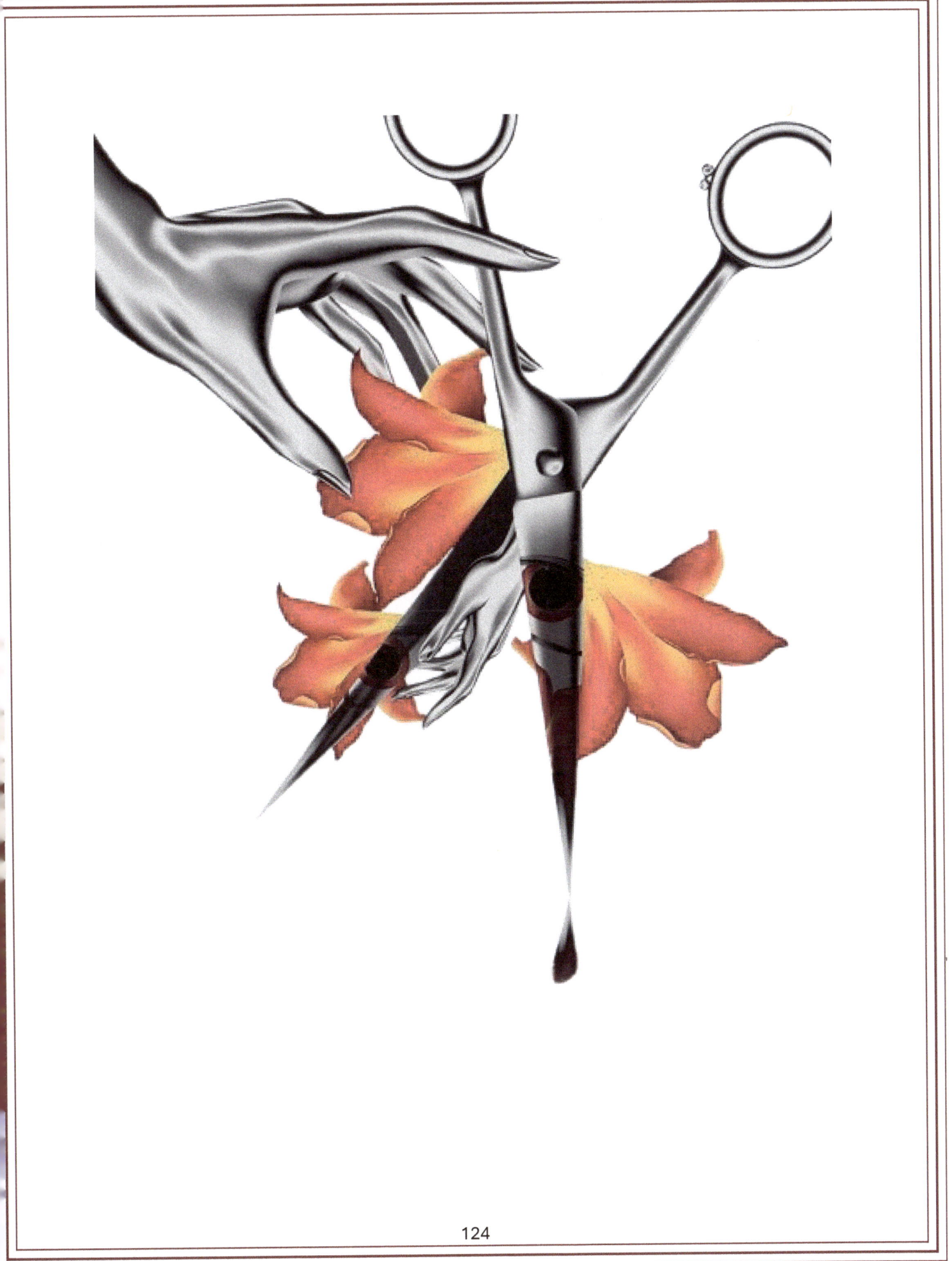

In My Head

In my bed,
In my head,
Things unsaid,
Left on read.

These feelings are too much,
I miss your touch,
You left me with a crutch,
Your disrespect came in clutch.

I took the bait,
I was too late,
So much hate,
Is this our fate?

The hate in your voice,
You hate me by choice,
There's too much noise,
To try to rejoice.

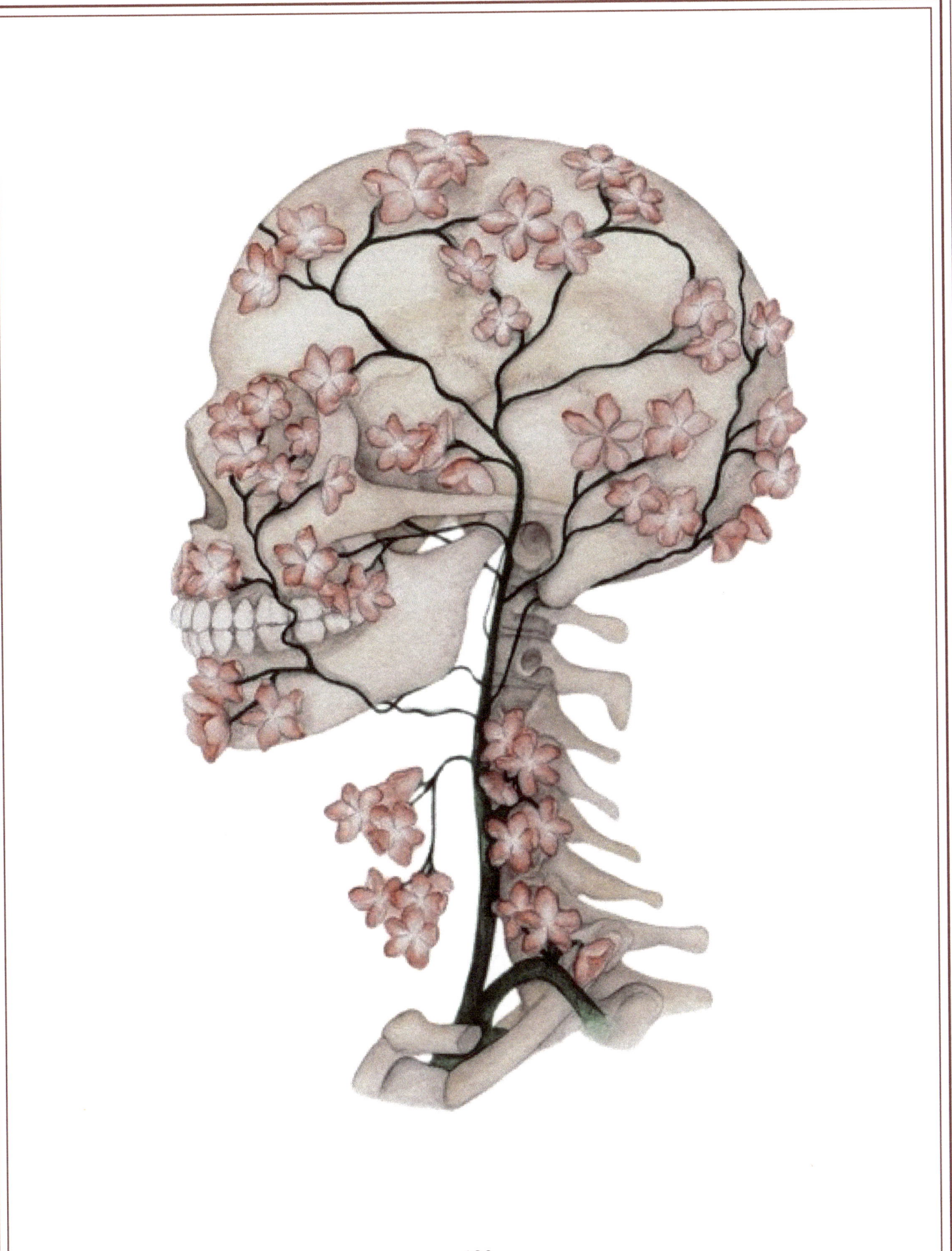

Here To Stay

His mind is constantly traveling
Searching for all the answers,
To all his problems
To all his cancers.
Why does he always think?
Is he on the brink?

He thinks of his trauma
Everything in his past,
He thinks of them everyday
Things that will always last.
What could he have done?
Was it that hard to save someone?

Was it his fault?
Was he to blame?
He tried to get help
But he still feels the same.
His trauma runs through his mind every day,
He wants it to stop but it's here to stay.

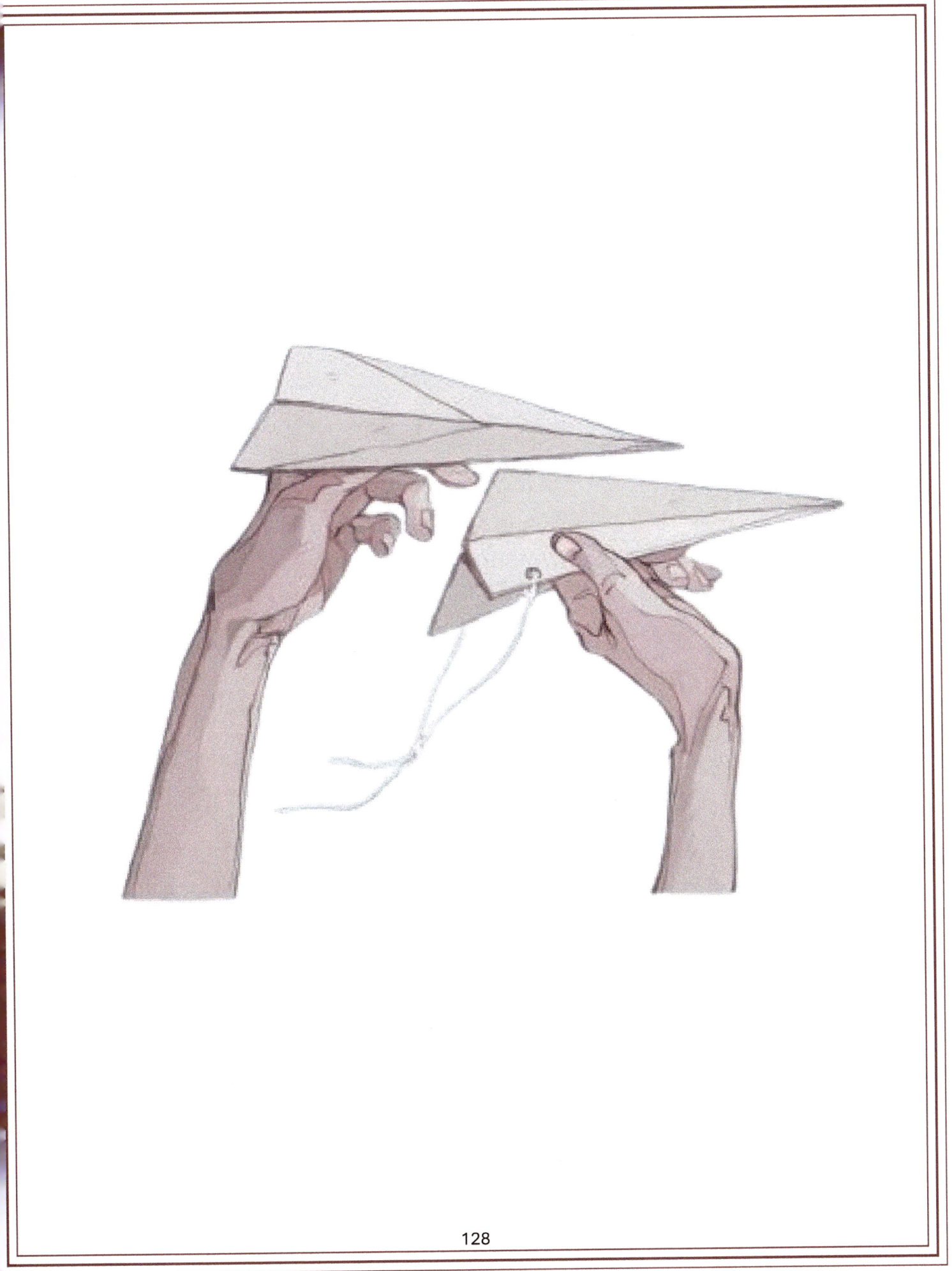

Leave Me Be

I wear my feelings
On my sleeve,
Of every emotion
That I believe.

It's too easy
For me to get hurt,
That's why I stay
Constantly alert.

I hate when people know
When I'm down,
I want to be left alone
Just let me drown.

There is peace
When I'm alone,
But calls keep coming
To my phone.

Leave me be
Let me suffer in silence,
Before I lose it
And resort to violence.

Prepare For War

If you want peace
Prepare for war,
I replay this quote
More and more.

I want peace
At least in my mind,
War with myself
Is the answer I find.

A war with the thoughts
A war with the voices,
A war with my trauma
A war with my choices.

Peace is my goal
Peace is the only option,
I'm prepared for war
Ready to proceed without cation.

My Creations

The words hit me
Like a train all at once,
Writing down things
I've thought of for moths.

The evil, the righteous,
The bad, and the good,
Form my stories
And thoughts I've withstood.

My mind constantly searches
For poems to put together,
Making pen to paper
And leaving me forever.

This is my therapy
It's how I survive,
Writing down my pains
Is what's keeping me alive.

My Addiction

My sadness pairs with depression,
It's always there, like an obsession.
I want to live in the fire, it's an addiction,
It feels good to me, it's my conviction.

My pain and my hurt fuel my motivation,
I'd like to be happy but it's not in the conversation.
I always wonder why I was made this way,
Is it something I did? Is it the things I say?

Joy is bliss so I create self-destruction,
It's the only way I've come to function.
Life goes to good, and I need to dismantle,
The emotions I feel are hard to handle.

I'd like an out, but I love it too much,
There's something about the excuse of having a crutch.
So, I'll continue to live in my own dysfunction,
Until my day comes where I feel compunction.

I Must Let You Go

I love you but I must let you go,
I know you can't forgive me for everything you know.
I've tried hard but nothing seems to work,
In my mind my feelings are going berserk.

It pains me to say,
Our love will never be the same way.
I did so much, there's no recovering from this,
I'd know what I'd ask for if I had one wish.

You and me together once again,
To forgive me for all my sin.
But for now, I know I must let you go,
I just wanted to say I love you one last time, so you know.

These Four Walls

Staring at these four walls
A little emptier now that you're gone,
You left because of me
From all that I did wrong.

It was all my anger
My self-destruction took over,
Since you've been gone
I've been sober.

I hope you come back
I hope I didn't take things too far,
Baby come back
You keep my life above par.

I'll let you in
I'll stay true to you,
I'm changing for us
I'll do whatever I have to do.

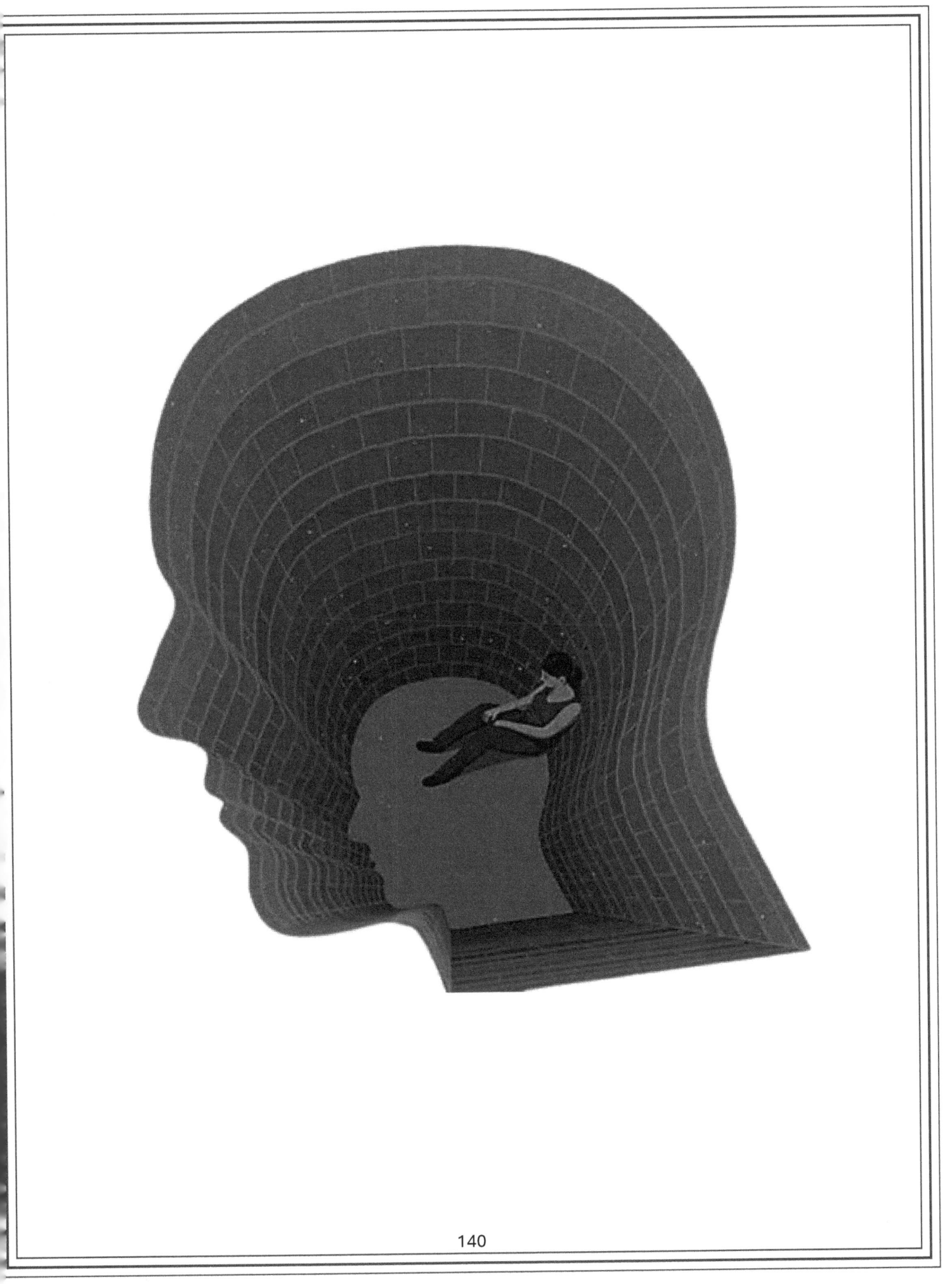

The, Is

The man I am
Is the man I want to be,
The love I feel
Is the love you will see.

The fear I have
Is the past I recognize,
The people I've lost
Is the reason I look to the skies.

The anxiety I have
Are the regrets of my behavior,
The way I pray
Is the way I ask for favor.

The thought of losing you
Is the reason I'm doing better,
The idea of being happy
Is the hope for me and you, forever.

www.ingramcontent.com/pod-product-compliance
Lightning Source LLC
Chambersburg PA
CBHW041116120626
46547CB00019B/2734